# Tools

One of the great things about crochet is that you need very few things to get going — just a crochet hook and some yarn and you are ready to go!

Like knitting needles, crochet hooks come in various sizes (diameters) — you'll find the size stamped on the flat thumb rest area around the middle of the hook. Hooks can come in wood, plastic or metal, and are also available with "comfort" handles — a soft area to grip around the middle of the hook — which are popular for those with arthritis, or who find their hands tire during long crochet sessions.

The size of the hook, as well as the yarn you use with it, will determine the size of the stitches it produces. The most common hook sizes are from 2-8mm, but finer hooks are used for intricate lace crochet work, while thicker hooks can be used in combination with thick jumbo yarn to crochet chunky items.

Metric(mm)	US hook	Old Uk hook
2.0	-	14
2.25	B/1	13
2.5	-	12
2.75	C/2	-
3	-	10
3.25	D/3	-
3.5	-	9
3.75	F/4	-
4.0	G/6	8
4.5	7	7
5.0	H/8	6
5.5	I/9	5
6	J/10	4
6.5	K/10.5	3
7	-	2
7.5	-	-
8.0	L/11	0
9.0	M/12	00
10.0	N/15	000

Most beginners will start with a size 4 or 5mm hook and a medium weight yarn — but for other projects see the chart on **page 6** for which hook to use with which yarn weight.

Other equipment:
It's always a good idea to have your sewing basket handy, with a pair of sharp scissors and some large darning needles for sewing up projects.

Yarns

When you first go shopping for yarn/wool you will notice that as well as a fantastic range of colours to choose from there is a dazzling array of types, thicknesses and weights available.

It's important to choose the correct weight of yarn for the project that you're making, and most patterns should tell you the size of needle to use **AND** the type or weight of yarn required.

Usually the weight or type of yarn is printed on the label — also known as the ball band — that is wrapped around it. The label will tell you the weight of the yarn, the tension, the washing instructions, and the most suitable needle size to use.

If you are crocheting a project that will use more than one ball of yarn, you should also check for the '**dye lot**' number on the band to ensure they are all the exact same colour.

	Lace	Super Fine	Fine	Light	Medium	Chunky
Yarn weight	0	1	2	3	4	5
Common use	Lace	Baby clothes, decorative items	Socks, baby clothes	Light scarves, accessories	Mittens, scarves, toys etc,	Blankets, scarves, winter items
Tension range (how many stitches per 10cm/4")	32–42 double crochets	21–32 sts	16–20 sts	12–17 sts	11–14 sts	8–11 sts
Recommended Hook Size (UK/US):	1.6–1.4 mm*/ 6, 7, 8, B–1* (* Steel)	2.25-3.5 mm/ B–1 to E–4	3.5-4.5 mm/ E–4 to 7	4.5-5.5 mm/ 7 to I–9	5.5-6.5 mm/ I–9 to K–10.5	6.5-9 mm/ K–10.5 to M–13

Easy E-Reader & Phone Covers

STITCH dc Double Crochet **USED**

These cute and cozy device cases are one of the quickest and easiest projects to crochet, so they're perfect for an absolute beginner. You simply crochet a basic square or rectangle and stitch it together to create the case.

For the cases in the photo I used a 5mm hook, together with the same chunky yarn as the neck wrap: *Rowan* "Big Wool" – a chunky 100% merino wool.

For a cute fastener, sew a button to the front of your case, then make a crochet chain long enough to loop around the button with both ends sewn securely to the back of the case.

As with the neck wrap, there is no strict pattern to follow – you can easily create a variety of covers based on the type of yarn you have available, and the measurements of your device. I used double crochet on these, but you can also try out other stitches if you like!

Measure the width of your device – then double it and add around 1cm/½ in. Remember that the crocheted yarn will stretch and you want the device to be held snugly within the case.

Chain 10 stitches to start with – wrap the chain length around your device – you want the first and last stitches to touch. If required, add one chain at a time until it fits around perfectly.

Then simply continue to work double crochet along each row, until your work is the same height as your device.

Don't forget your 'turning chain' for double crochet – chain 1 at the beginning of each new row.

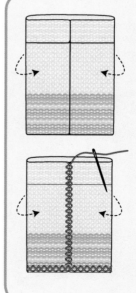

To sew up your case – see **page 20** – lay the finished work flat, with the nice side of the crochet facing up. Fold the left and right edges in to meet in the middle. Stitch these edges together, and also join the two bottom edges to create a 'case'. Turn right sides out and slip your device inside.

Baby Blanket

STITCH dc Double Crochet USED

The thought of crocheting an entire blanket can be daunting to a newcomer – but if you tackle it one square at a time it can be a great way to practice your crochet stitches and use up leftover yarn.

To ensure that each square is the same size, it's important to use the same weight of yarn and hook size for each.

If you're going to mix it up by having squares in a variety of stitches, make sure that each square is the same size by adjusting the number you chain for **each** stitch style.

This blanket used squares that began with a chain of 20, and used double crochet.

Work double crochet across each and every row. After about 10 rows, measure the width of your work. If the width was, say 15cm/6" then you should continue to crochet rows until the work reaches the same height as it is wide, so that you have a perfect square, then fasten off.

Keep crocheting squares until you have enough for the size of blanket you'd like, then stitch together using leftover yarn.

If you crocheted just one square per night, you could have a lovely blanket in just a few weeks!

Fingerless Mittens

So that they made a cute matching set, I used the same 5mm hook and chunky yarn as the neck wrap, but chose a lovely green colour.

I used double crochet again as it is a nice, dense stitch and ideal for winter garments, but you can try any stitch you like for these easy fingerless mittens.

You simply crochet a wide rectangle for each mitten, then fold over and stitch together – it couldn't be easier!

Chain 20. Check that the chain wraps all around the widest point of your hand – if not, add extra chain until it does.

Double crochet each row until you have created a wide rectangle that reaches from your knuckle area, down to about 2.5cm/1 in. below your wrist (see illustration below). Fasten off.

Repeat for second mitten, then sew each mitten together, inside out, following the illustrations below. Turn right sides out when finished.

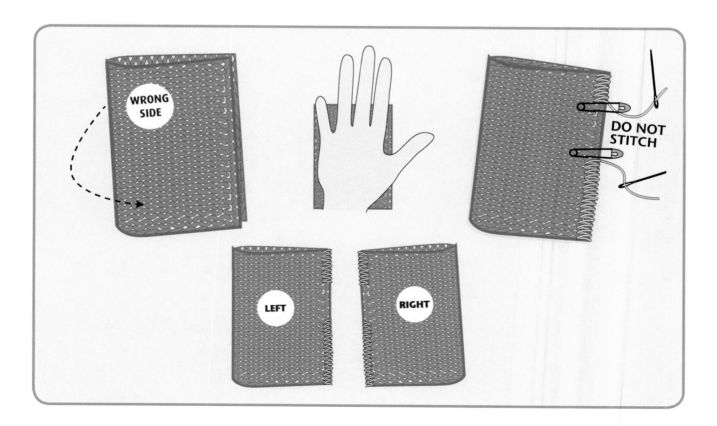

Baby Pom Pom Hat

STITCH
tr
Treble Crochet
USED

Time to crochet something for the little person in your life, and to try out a new stitch – treble crochet!

Unlike some hats which require lots of reducing, or crocheting 'in the round' – pretty complicated for a beginner – to create the shape, these lovely hats are made using two crocheted square panels, stitched together and gathered at the "ears". Tiny pom poms complete the look.

You will need:

1 x 100g ball of Soft Merino Aran (100% merino superwash)

4.5mm crochet hook

Tapestry needle

4 or 6 small pom poms
(2 or 3 for each side of hat)
5cm/2 in. diameter
– see **page 22**.

Size guide:

Newborn:
Chain 26.
Size of each panel = 18 x 18cm/7 x 7 in.

12 months:
Chain 34.
Size of each panel = 23 x 23cm/9 x 9 in.

Toddlers:
Chain 40.
Size of each panel = 26 x 26cm/10 x 10 in.

Check the size guide below and chain the correct size foundation chain.

See **page 16** for a reminder of how to do treble crochet.

Row 1: Treble crochet (**tr**) all the way to end of row.

Next row: Don't forget that treble crochet requires a TURNING CHAIN of 3 chain at the beginning of each new row.

Continue to work treble crochet (**tr**) along each row until your panel measures the correct size and is a square (height of work same as width). Fasten off.

Repeat to make a second identical panel.

Sewing up your hat:

Lay the first crocheted panel with the right side – what will ultimately be the *outside* of the hat – facing up. Now lay the second panel face down on top so that the "*right side*" of each panel is touching.

Make sure the foundation chain/bottom edge of each panel matches up. Starting on the left side sew both panels together – left side, across the top and right side, leaving the bottom seams open.

Turn the hat right sides out.

Thread a tapestry needle with spare yarn and use to gather the right corner of the hat before sewing the pom poms VERY securely to the hat. Repeat for left corner of hat.

Crochet Flowers

STITCH
dc
Double Crochet
USED

STITCH
tr
Treble Crochet
USED

These pretty flowers can be used to decorate many of the projects in this book – hats, scarves, gloves – or can be used to make pretty brooches or hair slides.

They're also a great way to use up leftover yarn – why not use a different colour for the inside and outside of each flower to really make them POP!

You will need:

4mm hook
Various light or medium-weight yarns

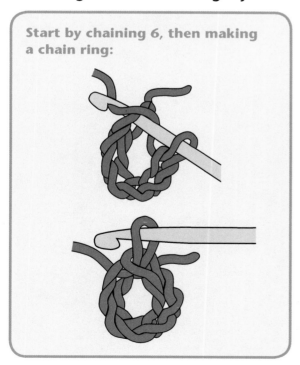

Start by chaining 6, then making a chain ring:

Inside of flower:

Chain 6 (**ch6**), then join into a ring by working a slip stitch – see **page 18** – into the first chain. You have now created a chain ring.

Now work a double crochet (**dc**) stitch into each stitch as you go around the chain ring, count until you have completed 16 double crochet (**16dc**) stitches. Work the tail of your yarn into each stitch as you go. Join the last stitch in by using a slip stitch (**ss**), then fasten off.

Outside of Flower:

Change yarn colour and join this in to the fastened-off stitch.

*Chain 3 (**ch3**), then work a treble crochet (**tr**) stitch into each of the next two stitches .

Chain 3 (**ch3**) again, then make a slip stitch (**ss**) into the next stitch.*

Repeat from * to * four more times – this will create five petals. Use a slip stitch (**ss**) to fasten off.

To create a full knot in the middle like the flowers in the picture, chain 10 (**ch10**) in a contrasting colour, twist the chain into a knot and stitch into the centre of your flower.

# Craft Basket

STITCH dc USED
Double Crochet

This cute and handy craft basket is an excellent way to master crocheting 'in the round' and is much easier than it looks. Can you believe it is actually crocheted altogether in just one piece?!

This pattern will make a basket 20cm/8in. in diameter, but you can adjust the pattern to make whatever size you wish.

You will need:

5mm crochet hook
2 x 100g balls of medium weight yarn

For the round base:

Centre round, Round 1: Begin with a foundation row of two chain stitches (**ch2**).

Skip the chain next to the hook and work a double crochet stitch into the next chain.

Then work five more double crochet stitches into the same chain – you've now worked a total of six stitches (**6dc**).

Join into a ring using a slip stitch (**ss**).

Round 2: You will now start to 'increase' your circle by working two double crochet stitches into each of the current six stitches (**12dc**). To do this, work a double crochet stitch into the next stitch along, then work another into the same stitch. Then do the same with each of the next five stitches.

Round 3: You should now make an increase into every other stitch. To do this do a regular double crochet into the first stitch (**1dc**), then two double crochet (**2dc**) into the next one, **1dc** into the next, **2dc** into the next and so on. At the end of this round you will now have 18 stitches.

With each additional round you crochet, you will continue to increase using the **2dc** method BUT the regularity will change. With each new round, add one to the number of double crochet solo stitches (**1dc**) you do in between each **2dc** increase i.e. in Round 3 you crocheted **2dc** into every other stitch

Round 4: 1dc, 1dc, 2dc, 1dc, 1dc, 2dc, (**2dc** into every 3rd stitch)

Round 5: 1dc, 1dc, 1dc, 2dc, 1dc, 1dc, 1dc, 2dc (**2dc** into every 4th stitch)

Round 6: 2dc into every 5th stitch and so on…

When your crocheted circle base has reached 20cm/8in. diameter (or your desired size), join the last stitch to the round with a slip stitch (**ss**).

Use a paper clip or stitch marker to mark the last stitch of each round, so you don't lose track of where you are!

For the sides of the basket:

Now that you have completed the round base you can start to crochet the "walls" of your basket.

Chain 1, then work a double crochet stitch into each stitch around the circle. Simply continue to work a double crochet (**1dc**) into each stitch until you have the height of basket you wish. Turning the top over like the basket in the photo can give it extra structure too!

Chick and Bunny Toys

STITCH
dc
Double Crochet
USED

How adorable are these little chicks and bunnies? Quick and easy to crochet, you can make them in a variety of colours, or even in stripes, and they make lovely gifts for the little people in your life.

The body of the toys are crocheted in one piece 'in the round', and involves some increasing and decreasing, so they're a great way to add to your crochet skills too!

You will need:

5mm crochet hook
1 x 50g ball of medium weight yarn
Tapestry needle
Toy filling
Black beads/buttons and tapestry thread for eyes/features

For the bunny/chick body:

Centre round, Round 1: Begin with a foundation row of two chain stitches (**ch2**). Skip the chain next to the hook and work a double crochet stitch into the next chain. Then work five more double crochet stitches into the same chain – you've now worked a total of six stitches (**6dc**). Join into a ring using a slip stitch (**ss**).

Round 2: You will now start to 'increase' your circle by working two double crochet stitches into each of the current six stitches (**12dc**). To do this, work a double crochet stitch into the next stitch along, then work another into the same stitch. Then do the same with each of the next five stitches.

Round 3: You should now make an increase into every other stitch. To do this do a regular double crochet into the first stitch (**1dc**) , then two double crochet (**2dc**) into the next one, **1dc** into the next, **2dc** into the next and so on. At the end of this round you will now have 18 stitches.

Round 4: 1dc, 1dc, 2dc, 1dc, 1dc, 2dc, (**2dc** into every 3rd stitch)

Round 5: 1dc, 1dc, 1dc, 2dc, 1dc, 1dc, 1dc,

Use a paper clip or stitch marker to mark the last stitch of each round, so you don't lose track of where you are!

2dc (**2dc** into every 4th stitch)

Rounds 6 – 14: 1dc into every stitch

Now it's time to start **DECREASING** our stitches to create the other end of the oval shape.

Round 15: * **1dc** into first three stitches, then double crochet the next two stitches together (**dc2tog**)*. Repeat from * to *. You now have 24 stitches.

Round 16: * **1dc** into first two stitches, then double crochet the next two stitches together (**dc2tog**)*. Repeat from * to *. You now have 18 stitches.

Round 17: * **1dc** into first stitch, then double crochet the next two stitches together (**dc2tog**)*. Repeat from * to *. You now have 12 stitches. At this point, use the opening to stuff the body of your bunny/chick with cotton toy filling.

To finish: Now **dc2tog** into every pair of stitches until the hole closes up. Pull tight, fasten off the yarn leaving a tail, and use the tapestry needle to sew the hold closed tightly.

For the bunny ears:

Step 1: Begin with a foundation row of two chain stitches (**ch2**). Skip the chain next to the hook and work a double crochet stitch into the next chain.

Then work five more double crochet stitches into the same chain – you've now worked a total of six stitches (**6dc**). Join into a ring using a slip stitch (**ss**).

Step 2: Work two double crochet stitches into each of the current six stitches (**12dc**). To do this, work a double crochet stitch into the next stitch along, then work another into the same stitch. Then do the same with each of the next five stitches. You now have 12 stitches.

Rounds 3-14: 1dc into every stitch. Finish with a slip stitch (**ss**) then fasten off, leaving a tail. Use your tapestry needle to gather the bottom of the ear and sew tightly to the bunny head.

Repeat all of the above to make the second ear.

For the bunny feet/chick wings:

Follow Steps 1 and 2 for the bunny ears. Then for five rows, work 1dc into each stitch. Finish with a slip stitch (**ss**) then fasten off, leaving a tail. Use your tapestry needle to gather the raw end of the foot/wing and sew tightly to the toy.

Dc2tog

Begin a double crochet stitch as usual:

· Hook through stitch, **yrh**, draw through loop. 2 loops on hook.

· Hook through the next stitch, **yrh**, draw through. 3 loops on hook.

· **Yrh**, draw through all 3 stitches. 1 loop on hook. Two stitches have now become one.

Hanging Hearts

STITCH dc Double Crochet **USED**

Just how gorgeous are these little hanging hearts? You can fill them with lavender to make a scented wardrobe hanger or drawer freshener, crochet in baby colours as a lovely newborn gift, or simply make lots and lots for friends. These are very easy to crochet and a great way to use up any lovely leftover yarn you have.

You will need:

1 x 50g ball of Soft Merino Aran (100% merino superwash)

3.5mm crochet hook

Toy filling

Lavender (optional)

Ribbon for hanging

Tapestry needle

Makes several hearts, each approx 10cm/4in diameter

For each side of your heart (make two):

Start with a foundation chain of two (**ch2**).

Work two double crochet stitches into the first stitch (**2dc**) then a regular double crochet stitch (**2dc**) into the next. You now have three stitches.

Remember with double crochet you have to do a turning chain of 1 at the beginning of each new row. This will be shown as **Ch1**.

Ch1. Work two double crochet stitches into the first stitch (**2dc**) then a regular double crochet stitch (**2dc**) into the next two stitches. You now have 4 stitches. Then:

Ch1. 2dc into the first stitch, then **1dc** into the next 3 stitches = 5 stitches.

Ch1. 2dc into the first stitch, then **1dc** into the next 4 stitches = 6 stitches.

Ch. Continue to double crochet every row,

increasing by doing a **2dc** into the first stitch of every row until you have 20 stitches.

Now to create one side of the rounded part of the heart:

Ch1, then work a double crochet stitch into 10 of the stitches only.

*Double crochet stitches 1 and 2 together (**2dctog** - see below), double crochet each of the next 6 stitches, then **2dctog** stitches 9 and 10.

For the next four rows, double crochet together the first two and the last two stitches of each row, and work a regular double crochet to the stitches in between. This will continue to reduce the stitches by two at a time and create the top curve of the heart. Once you have two stitches left, fasten off.*

Now to create the second round part of the heart:

Re-attach your yarn in the 11th stitch of the 20 stitches row (right next to the first round part) work a double crochet into each of the 10 stitches. Then continue as above, from * to *. Leave a tail of yarn for sewing up the heart.

Once you have crocheted both sides of your heart, stitch together, inside out to hide the stitches. Begin near the bottom of one of the straight sides, this allows you to leave a small opening – turn the heart right sides out, lightly stuff with toy filling and some scented lavender if you wish. Stitch closed and add pretty ribbon for hanging.

Dc2tog

Begin a double crochet stitch as usual:

· Hook through stitch, **yrh**, draw through loop. 2 loops on hook.

· Hook through the next stitch, **yrh**, draw through. 3 loops on hook.

· Yrh, draw through all 3 stitches. 1 loop on hook. Two stitches have now become one.

Granny Squares

STITCH tr Treble Crochet USED

STITCH htr Half Treble Crochet USED

If you had to choose just one item that represented "crochet", then it could only be the traditional 'granny square'!

Once you start making these, you'll quickly become hooked – they're a great way to use up leftover yarn, can be made in all one colour or a cool mix of colours, and squares can be joined together to make scarves, bags, cushions and blankets. Why not start with one and see where it takes you?!

You will need:
Leftover yarn in various colours– medium weight
4.5mm crochet hook

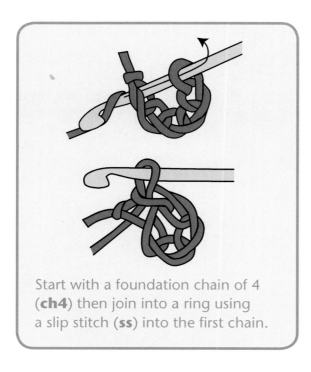
Start with a foundation chain of 4 (**ch4**) then join into a ring using a slip stitch (**ss**) into the first chain.

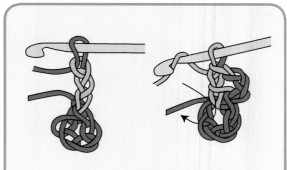
Chain 3 (**ch3**), then work two treble stitches into the ring. Notice that in order to go "under" each stitch, the hook is actually reaching inside the ring.

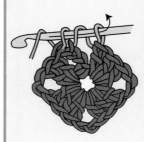
Chain 2 (**ch2**), then work three trebles into the ring. Repeat this process three times. You have now worked four 'sets'. Can you see your first small square forming? To join the square together, work a half-treble stitch (see **page 14**) into the third chain from the very beginning – see diagram.

Now it's time to add another layer to our granny square – if you wish, change yarn colour now (see **page 19**).

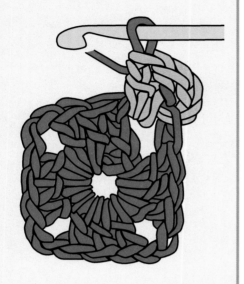

Chain 3 (**ch3**), then work two trebles into the chain space.

With granny squares, the unique patterns are formed using clusters of stitches and chains which also create spaces – called chain spaces. So, unlike other types of crochet, you may need to work your stitches into the chain space not the actual chain itself.

Chain 1 (**ch1**), work three trebles into the chain space. Chain 2 (**ch2**), work three trebles. Insert hook into the next chain space.

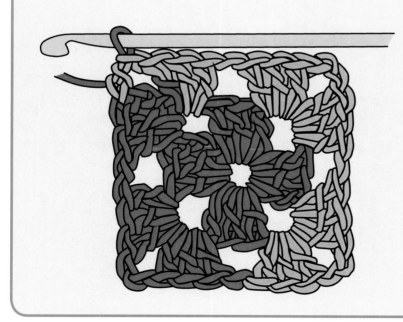

*Chain 1 (**ch1**), work three trebles into the chain space. Chain 2 (**ch2**), work three trebles.

Insert hook into the next chain space*.

Repeat from * to * , then join all together using a half-treble into the 3rd chain of the first 3 chain.

Congratulations! – you've just finished your first granny square!

More great Craft books from Kyle Craig

I hope you've enjoyed learning to Crochet. Why not learn some new Sewing or Knitting skills with the help of my other books:

Adult Beginner's Books

How To Knit:
A Complete Guide for Absolute Beginners

How To Crochet:
A Complete Guide for Absolute Beginners

How To Use Your Sewing Machine:
A Complete Guide for Absolute Beginners

Kids Books

My First Knitting Book

My First Crochet Book

My First Sewing Book

My First Hand Sewing Book

My First Sewing Machine Book

My First Sewing Machine: Fashion School

Search under Alison McNicol for tons more great adult and kids craft books!

Introduction

Welcome to How To Crochet: A Complete Guide for Absolute Beginners.

Crochet has risen hugely in popularity in recent years and, as with knitting, is no longer seen as an 'old granny' pastime. A whole new generation of young women — and perhaps even men! — are discovering how fun and easy it is to pick up a crochet hook and some yarn and create something beautiful.

This book is aimed at the absolute beginner, so don't worry if you have never tried to crochet before — the clear and easy to follow illustrations and pictures here will help you get started and have you crocheting your first stitches in no time.

The names of the basic crochet stitches are different in the USA and UK, so we have provided BOTH names at the top of each new stitch page. To avoid confusion, the PROJECTS instructions use just the UK names. See page 23 for more crochet terminology.

I've chosen a lovely selection of projects that are easy enough for complete novices to make in a relatively short space of time, and that progress your skills as you move on through the book – so whether you're hoping to make cute crocheted gifts for friends, beautiful baby hats or accessories for loved ones, or have your heart set on a big granny square blanket, there's sure to be a project here to inspire you.

So — what are you waiting for? Read on, follow the steps provided, and you'll be delighted to discover just how easy it is to learn to crochet!

Happy crocheting!

Alison x

Contents

Holding the Hook

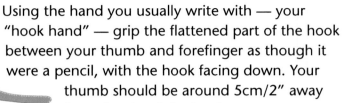

Using the hand you usually write with — your "hook hand" — grip the flattened part of the hook between your thumb and forefinger as though it were a pencil, with the hook facing down. Your thumb should be around 5cm/2" away from the tip of the hook.

Left Handed crocheters: hold the hook the exact same way in your left hand.

Holding the Yarn

There are lots of ways of controlling the yarn while you crochet, and after a while you will find what works best for you. Try this technique to start with **[a]**:

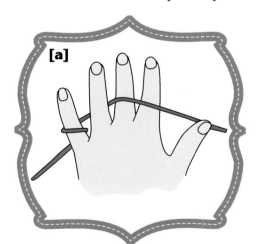

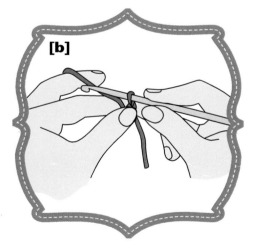

The hand that is not holding the hook will be called your "yarn hand". Release a decent amount of yarn from the ball and start by winding it around your little finger. Next, pass it under the next finger along, bringing it out over your middle and index fingers.

In a moment you will learn how to make a slip knot to start, then you'll be ready to use both hands, in position like this **[b]**, to start to crochet.

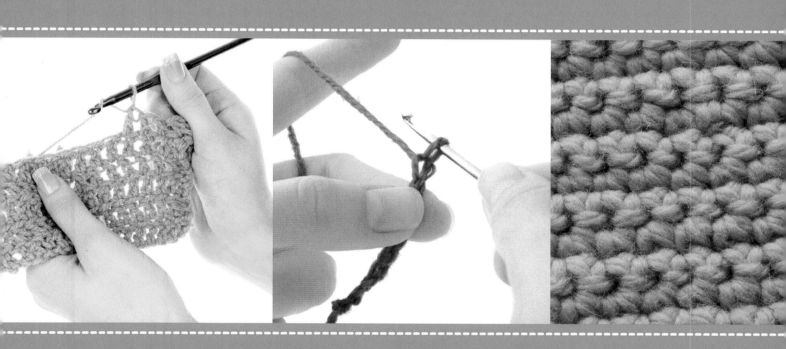

Stitches

The names of the basic crochet stitches are different in the USA and UK, so we have provided BOTH names at the top of each new stitch page.

UK stitch name	Abbreviation	US stitch name
Double crochet	**dc**	Single crochet
Treble crochet	**tr**	Double crochet
Half Treble	**htr**	Half Double
Double Treble	**dtr**	Treble

Making a Slip Knot

All crochet work begins with a slip knot which acts as your first stitch and can be tightened or loosened easily.

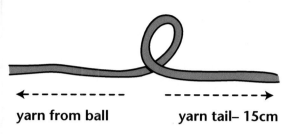

← - - - - - - - - - - - → ← - - - - - - - - - →
yarn from ball   yarn tail– 15cm

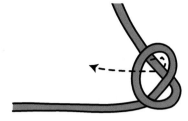

Step 1: First make a loop, about 15cm in from the tail end of the yarn.

Step 2: Now pull the "working" end of the yarn (the yarn that leads to the ball) through the loop.

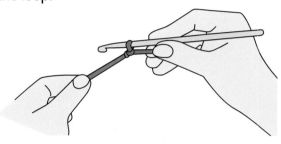

Step 3: This new loop is now your slip knot.

Step 4: Now slip your crochet hook through this loop and pull gently on both ends of the yarn to tighten the loop. It should still be able to move freely up and down your hook, otherwise it is too tight.

On a crochet pattern you will see the term **yrh** which means "yarn over hook".

Yarn Over Hook

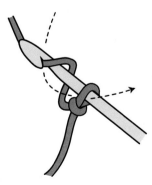

Step 1: Crocheting consists of a series of loops, created using your yarn and hook to pull one loop through the next. Keeping the notch on the hook facing down will allow you to "catch" the yarn with the hook each time.

Step 2: Bring the yarn over the hook towards you then, catching it on the hook, dip the hook down and through the loop on the hook, as shown by the arrow.

Chain Stitch

Chain stitch is the first, and most basic, of all crochet stitches. Most crochet patterns will begin by creating a certain number of chain stitches.

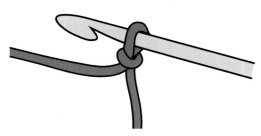

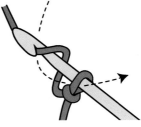

Step 1: Hands in the starting position, slip knot on hook.

Step 2: Yarn over hook, pull through to create 1 chain.

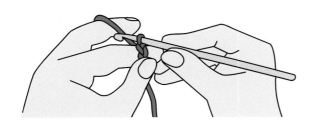

Step 3: Gently pinch the chain stitch you've just made, and repeat.

Step 4: Continue as above until you have counted the correct number of chain stitches. The slip stitch does not count. Lost track? See below for how to count chain stitches.

Checking Your Tension

TOO TIGHT

IDEAL TENSION

TOO LOOSE

Counting Chain Stitches

Front of chain

Back of chain

| 5 | 4 | 3 | 2 | 1 |

Count each stitch (using front of chain)

Double Crochet Stitch

 USA stitch name: **Single Crochet Stitch**

Double crochet is one of the easiest crochet stitches to do, and many of the projects in this book will use this to help get you started. It creates quite a chunky, dense pattern, so is ideal for winter accessories and toys.

To practice the stitch, let's start with a chain (**ch**) of 15 stitches.

Step 1: Insert your hook into the second stitch from the hook. You should see the two strands – the 'V'– of the stitch on top of your hook. Wrap the yarn over the hook (**yrh**), then pull through the chain. You will now have two loops on your hook.

Step 2: Yarn over hook (**yrh**), then pull through both stitches.

Step 3: You now have one loop on your hook and have completed your first double crochet stitch!

Step 4: Continue by working a double crochet stitch into each chain until you reach the end. Count to ensure you now have 14 stitches – see **page 11**.

ch
= chain

yrh
= yarn over hook

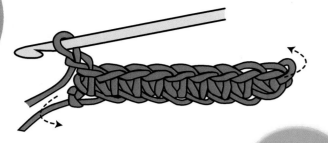

Step 5: Now make a "turning chain" by chaining one stitch (**ch 1**), then turning your work around so that you are ready to begin the next row. (Most crochet stitches will have a very crucial "turning chain" of one or more stitches, which will depend on the height of the stitch, that you must do at the start of each new row.)

TURNING =1 CHAIN

Step 6: Start the next row by inserting your hook under the top two threads of the next stitch along, then continue to double crochet to the end again. Then check the number of stitches – at first it can be easy to miss the final stitch in the row!

Check your stitches!

Count your stitches at the end of each row. If you look at the top of each stitch, you will see a V shape. Count each V – if you began with a chain of 15 you should now have 14 stitches at the end of each row.

Half Treble Stitch

 USA stitch name: **Half Double Stitch**

Once you are working double crochet stitches with confidence, you're ready to try Half Treble Stitch! The result is not quite as dense as double crochet, so it is slightly softer, and is ideal for warm clothing and baby/children's clothes and accessories.

To practice the stitch, let's start with a chain (**ch**) of 15 stitches.

Remember how to count chains!

Step 1: First, wrap the yarn over the hook (**yrh**) *before* you go into the chain. Then insert your hook into the third chain along from the hook. Yarn over hook (**yrh**) again, then pull through the chain.

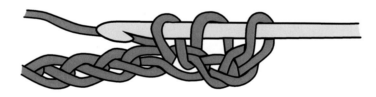

Step 2: You now have three loops on your hook.

Step 3: Yarn over hook (**yrh**) and pull your hook through all three stitches.

Step 4: You now have one loop on your hook and have completed your first half treble crochet stitch!

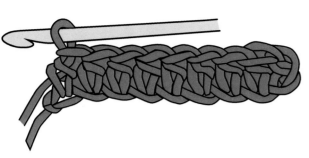

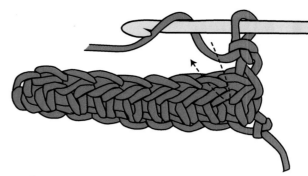

Step 5: Continue by working a half treble stitch into each chain until you reach the end.

Step 6: As you did in double crochet, now make a "turning chain"– for this stitch you need to chain 2 (**ch 2**) before each new row. Now turn your work around so that you are ready to begin the next row. Then it's yarn over hook (**yrh**), slip your hook under the very next stitch, yarn over hook (**yrh**), pull through all three stitches, and so on.

TURNING **=2** CHAIN

Don't forget to always put your hook under BOTH of the top two threads of the stitch!

Treble Crochet Stitch

 USA stitch name: **Double Crochet Stitch**

Treble crochet is a less dense and more open stitch than the double crochet and half treble crochet you have tried so far. This makes it even softer, and ideal for baby or summer garments. It is also quite a tall stitch, so you will be quick to see results with each new row you crochet!

To practice the stitch, let's start with a chain (**ch**) of 15 stitches.

Step 1: To start the stitch, and as you did to start a half treble, wrap the yarn over the hook (**yrh**) *before* you go into the chain. Then insert your hook into the fourth chain along from the hook. Yarn over hook (**yrh**) again, then pull through the chain.

Step 2: You now have three loops on your hook.

Step 3: Yarn over hook (**yrh**), then pull hook through two of the loops only.

Step 4: You now have two loops on your hook.

Step 5: Yarn over hook (**yrh**), then pull hook through the two loops.

Step 6: You now have one loop remaining and have now completed your first treble stitch!

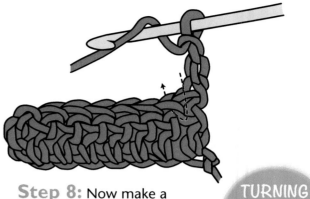

Step 7: Continue by working a treble stitch into each chain until you reach the end

Step 8: Now make a "turning chain" – for this stitch you need to chain 3 (**ch 3**) before each new row. Now turn your work around so that you are ready to begin the next row. Then it's yarn over hook (**yrh**), slip your hook under the very next stitch, and pull through. Then continue from Step 2.

TURNING
=3
CHAIN

Slip Stitch

A slip stitch is the shortest of all crochet stitches and can be used for a variety of purposes, depending on the pattern. Slip stitches can be used as the last stich on a row to create a smooth end, to join ends in circular crochet, to join in new yarn, or simply to move your hook to a new position.

Step 1: Put your hook through the next stitch, then yarn over hook (**yrh**).

Step 2: Pull yarn through the work **AND** the original loop at the same time. Your slip stitch is now complete.

Increase/Decrease

To create 'shapes' in your crochet work, you may at times need to increase or decrease the number of stitches in the row that you are working on.

Your pattern will usually tell you how many stitches to crochet together i.e.

dc2tog =
double crochet 2 together

dc3tog =
double crochet 3 together

tr3tog =
treble crochet 3 together

and so on...

Decreasing

Regardless of the actual stitch you are using, the basic technique for decreasing remains the same – you will crochet two or more stitches together to reduce them down to one stitch.

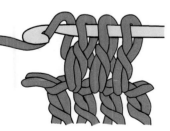

Here we wanted to work three treble stitches together (**tr3tog**). Work a treble stitch into each of three stitches as normal, but leave the last loop of each on the hook. You will be left with three loops on the hook. Yarn over hook (**yrh**), and pull through all three stitches. You will then be left with 1 loop on your hook. To **dc2tog**, see **page 42**.

Increasing

To increase your row by a stitch, you will work two or three stitches into same stitch. Here we have crocheted two stitches into the same stitch. Work one stitch as normal. Insert your hook into the stitch you have just worked and do a second stitch. You have now increased your row by one stitch.

Joining Yarn

Whether starting a new ball of yarn, or joining in a new colour, the technique for joining in is the same. Always make the change at the beginning of a new row.

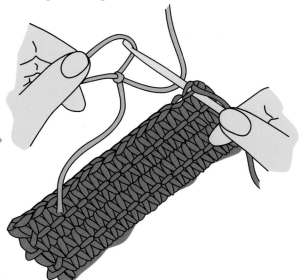 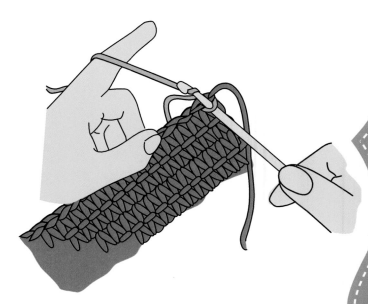

Step 1: Fasten off the first colour – see below. Now make a slip knot with the new colour. Insert your hook through the first stitch of the row, then slip the slip knot over your hook.

Step 2: Draw the new colour through the stitch. Yarn over hook (**yrh**) and work one chain stitch – this will secure the new colour, then continue to work your stitches as normal.

Fastening Off

At the end of your piece of crochet, it's important to 'fasten off' your stitches correctly to stop your work unravelling.

Cut your yarn, leaving a tail of around 10cm/4 in. Loosen the loop of the last stitch, then pull the end of the yarn through that loop all the way, and tighten. You may then want to leave a tail of yarn long enough to sew the item together.

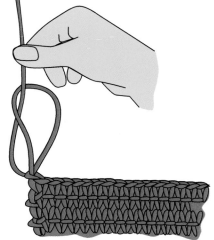

Sewing Together

Once you have crocheted all the parts of a project, it will be time to sew them together. Usually you will want your stitches to be hidden, so you should use a large darning or tapestry needle and the same yarn to sew the pieces together.

You may already know some sewing stitches, but here's a new one used especially in crochet and knitting – **mattress stitch**. This stitch is a great way to sew together crocheted pieces as invisibly as possible. When sewing crochet together, always use a large tapestry needle (make sure your tapestry needle is blunt to avoid piercing the yarn).

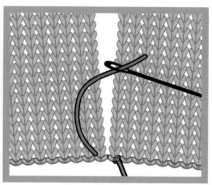

Step 1: Lay the pieces you wish to join on a flat surface, side by side, with the *wrong side,* (the inside) facing up. Thread your needle with the same yarn, then secure it to the end of your crocheted work with a couple of stitches on top of each other.

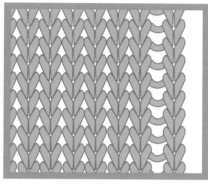

Step 2: Now look closely at the crochet and gently pull apart the first two edge stitches. Can you see the series of little horizontal running threads connecting them? We will be using these for our mattress stitches.

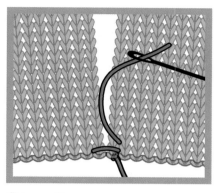

Step 3: Put your needle under and through the horizontal running thread that runs between the first and second stitch on the opposite piece of crochet, like in this diagram. Pull your yarn all the way through.

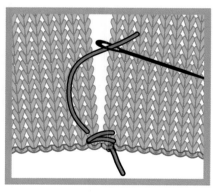

Step 4: Cross over to the other piece of crochet and do the same, on the same stitch, on that side. Pull the yarn through again. Carry on like this, zig zagging from one piece to the other, moving up one stitch each time.

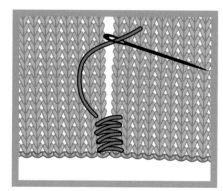

Step 5: Each time you make a stitch and pull on the yarn tight, you will be creating a strong "seam" to hold your work together. When you reach the end, secure with 2 or 3 stitches on top of each other.

The **RIGHT SIDE** is the side of your crocheted piece that you want on display. The **WRONG SIDE** will be the back, or the inside, of your crocheted item.

Sewing On Buttons

Once you have crocheted something, you may want to add buttons to look like eyes, or just to make it prettier.

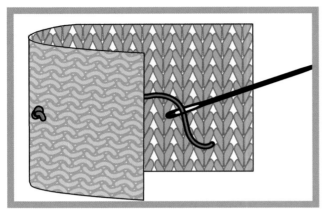

Step 1: Thread your needle with matching yarn or thread and tie a knot at the far end. (Before doing this, double check that the eye of your needle fits through the holes in your button. If not, use a smaller needle!) Decide where you want your button to be, and bring your needle up through the middle of that area, from the rear of the crochet so that the needle comes out on the **RIGHT** side.

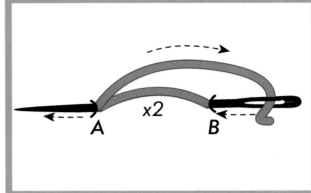

Step 2: Now sew two small stitches on top of each other. This will secure your thread or yarn to the crochet before you start sewing on your button.

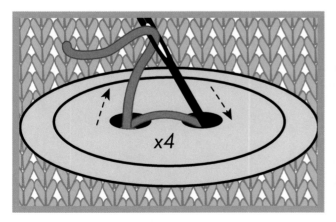

Step 3: Grab your button and place it over the area it will go. Now bring your needle and thread up through one hole of the button. Pull thread all the way. Next go down through the other hole, again pulling thread all the way. Do this 4 times, or until it no longer feels wobbly when you tug on it.

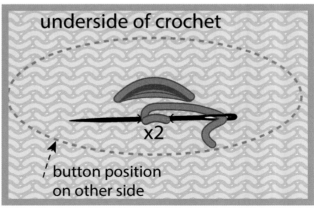

Step 4: On the underside of the crochet, just underneath where the button now is, do two or three small stitches to secure your thread or yarn. You have now sewn on your button and can cut the extra yarn off. Be **VERY** careful not to cut into your crochet!

Making Pom Poms

Pom Poms are so fun and easy to make and can be used on all sorts of projects – on hats, scarves, bags and more!

All you need is some cardboard and yarn, and some round lids or shapes to draw around, and you're all set!

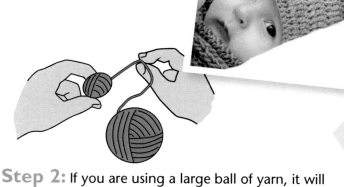

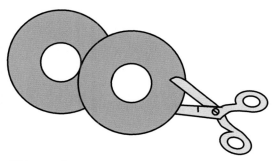

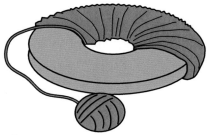

Step 1: How large would you like your pom pom? Find a jar lid, CD or something of similar size and draw around it on the cardboard. Now draw a smaller circle inside the large one. Repeat this, so that you cut two cardboard "donuts" that are both the same.

Step 2: If you are using a large ball of yarn, it will be too big to pass through the hole, so make a small ball that will fit by winding the yarn around your fingers lots of times. Stop before it is too large to fit through the hole.

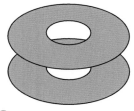

Step 3: Now put both discs together. You're now ready to start winding your yarn around the discs.

Step 4: Holding the two discs together, start winding your yarn over the disc and through the hole, repeating again and again until you have covered the whole disc in yarn. Keep repeating this until the hole is too small for any more yarn to pass through.

Step 5: Carefully insert one blade of your scissors between the two discs, and start cutting through the yarn. Keep moving the scissors around the edge, cutting the yarn as you go, until you have cut all the way around.

Step 6: Cut a length of yarn and carefully pull apart the two discs slightly. Wrap your yarn between the two discs and around the middle of your pom pom, and tie in a tight knot. Do this a couple more times so that your pom pom is really secure. Now rip or cut each disc away, and roll your pom pom between your hands to hide the join and make it nice and fluffy!

Understanding Crochet Terminology

Once you move on from this book, regular crochet patterns or instructions will feature a host of abbreviations and crochet terminology. We will use them, together with fuller explanations, throughout this book to get you used to them and prepare you for regular patterns.

The names for the basic stitches are different in the UK to the US, so it's important to know the origins of any book or pattern you are using to ensure you use the correct stitch. This book uses the UK terminology throughout – for US readers, please see the US names below.

UK stitch name	Abbreviation	US stitch name
Double crochet	**dc**	Single crochet
Treble crochet	**tr**	Double crochet
Half Treble	**htr**	Half Double
Double Treble	**dtr**	Treble

Crochet Terminology

Foundation chain
This is the base chain of stitches that you create and work the first row of crochet stitches into.

Foundation row
The first row of stitches worked into the foundation chain.

Skip a stitch
Miss the next stitch along and work into the one after that.

Turning chain
The extra chain stitches that you work at the beginning of a new row to bring your hook/work up to the correct height for the next stitch. Each stitch may require a different number of turning chain stitches.

Dc2tog — work two double crochet stitches together
Insert hook into next stitch along, **yrh** (yarn over hook) draw loop through. Do not finish double crochet stitch, instead insert hook into next stitch along, **yrh**, pull loop through. You now have three loops on your hook. **Yrh**, then pull through all three stitches.

Dc3tog — work three double crochet stitches together
As above but do this for three stitches in a row, which will result in four loops on your hook. **Yrh** then draw through all four loops.

Abbreviations

alt	alternate		**inc**	increase
beg	beginning		**oz**	ounce
ch	chain		**rep**	repeat
cm	centimetres		**ss**	slip stitch
cont	continue / continuing		**st(s)**	stitch(es)
dec	decrease		**tog**	together
in	inches		**yrh**	yarn over hook

Projects

The stitch names featured in each project refer to the UK name. Please see page 23 for equivalent US names.

Chunky Neck Wrap

STITCH
dc
Double Crochet
USED

For your very first project we're going to crochet something that doesn't require you to follow a complicated, rigid pattern. This will allow you to practice crocheting and get used to holding your hook, tensioning your yarn and perfecting your first crochet stitch – double crochet. Check back to **page 12** for double crochet instructions.

Choose a yarn you like – for scarves and wraps like this a chunky yarn is a great choice PLUS it crochets up much quicker than a finer yarn. Pick a hook size to match your yarn – **see page 6** – for a chunky yarn like this we used a size 5mm hook.

The neck wrap here was crocheted using a 5mm hook and 1 x 100g ball of Rowan "Big Wool" a chunky 100% merino wool. I "chained 20" for the foundation chain, then used Double Crochet – dc – stitch throughout. The finished length – from one whole ball of yarn – is 80cm/32 in.

Chain 20 stitches to start with (**ch20**) – the thickness of your yarn will determine the size of the chain, and therefore the width of your neck wrap. Hold the chain length against you – is it as wide as you would like your wrap to be? If not, chain more stitches.

Then simply continue to work double crochet along each row, until the wrap is the required length – check regularly by holding against you.

Don't forget your 'turning chain' for double crochet – chain 1 at the beginning of each new row.

Sew in a hidden press-stud or pieces of Velcro/hook'n'loop to hold the wrap in place when wearing. You could even sew on a decorative button to give the impression of a buttonhole!

If the above were a standard pattern it could look like this:

Using a 5mm hook and chunky yarn, ch20.

Row 1: Ch1, dc to the end, turn.

Rep this row until the wrap/scarf is desired length. Fasten off yarn.

How To
CROCHET

A Complete Guide
for Absolute Beginners

Alison McNicol

First published in 2013 by Kyle Craig Publishing

Text and illustration copyright © 2013 Kyle Craig Publishing

Design and illustration: Julie Anson

ISBN : ISBN: 978-1-908707-24-6
A CIP record for this book is available from the British Library.

A Kyle Craig Publication
www.kyle-craig.com